Sam was on the hill.

The fog got bad.

Sam saw Kim in the fog.

But it was not Kim. It was a bush.

Sam saw Kev in the fog.

But it was not Kev. It was a sack.

Sam saw Grandad in the fog.

But it was not Grandad.
It was a tree.

"What is **that**?" said Sam.
"It is **not** a bush. It is **not** a sack. It is **not** a tree."

"It's a bull!" said Sam. "It's a big bull!"

"It's a big, bad bull! said Sam. "Help!"

Sam ran and ran. So did the big, bad bull.

Sam hid. So did the big, bad bull.

"Yap, yap, yap!" said the big, bad bull.

"You are not a big, bad bull," said Sam.

"You are a big, bad Rags!"